To Andrea
Love
Uncle Brian
Aunt Louise
Jennifer + Steven

Translated by Anthea Bell

British Library Cataloguing in Publication Data
Bolliger, Max
 The magic bird.
 I. Title II. Lenica, Jan III. Der
bunte Vogel. *English*
833'.914[J] P27
ISBN 0-86264-146-2

Text © 1986 by Max Bolliger. Illustrations © 1986 by Jan Lenica. First published in Great Britain in 1986 by Andersen Press Limited, 62-65 Chandos Place, London WC2. Published in Australia by Century Hutchinson Australia Pty. Limited, Hawthorn, Victoria 3122. First published by Bohem Press, Zürich, Switzerland as *Der bunte Vogel.* All rights reserved.
Printed in Italy by Grafiche AZ, Verona.

Max Bolliger
Jan Lenica

The Magic Bird

Andersen Press · London

A giant and a dwarf once lived together in a great forest.
They were very old.
They were the last giant and the last dwarf in the world.

Each felt lonely, in his own way:
one in a noisy way,
the other in a quiet way.
But what they both wanted most of all
was to be like those creatures
known as Men.

However, if you think
the giant and the dwarf
were a comfort to each other,
you are much mistaken.
The older they grew
the more they quarrelled
and the more they tormented one another.

The giant shook his gigantic fist
at the dwarf,
blew in his face
and sent him flying through the air.

And when the dwarf landed
on top of a tree,
the giant laughed and laughed
at the trouble he had scrambling down again.

As for the dwarf,
he put out his tiny tongue at the giant,
and called him rude names.

Sometimes he crept up behind the giant
and pinched him,
and he laughed and laughed
to see the giant look for the culprit in vain.

But all the same,
they stayed together.
They needed one another,
because they had nobody else
to shake their fists at
or to call rude names.
The forest creatures
had taken to avoiding
the pair of them.

One day they found
a tiny bird.

Not a blackbird.
Not a woodpecker.
Not a jay.
It was an ordinary, grey little bird,
a bird without a name.

It lay on the ground,
looking imploringly at them
with its round little eyes.

They picked the bird up,
built it a nest,
gave it food
and gave it drink.
They took turns
to watch over the bird
and protect it
from its enemies.

The dwarf was surprised
to see how gently the giant
stroked the bird
with his huge hands.
And the giant was surprised
to see how comfortingly
the sharp-tongued dwarf
talked to the bird.

The giant and the dwarf
were kept so busy
looking after the orphaned bird
that they quite forgot
to quarrel
and torment each other.

Meanwhile, the bird
was getting a little stronger
day by day.
And when he began
to flap his wings,
the giant and the dwarf saw,
to their surprise,
that all his feathers
had turned different colours.

They were so fascinated
by the sight
of those brightly coloured feathers,
that they never noticed how they,
as well as the bird,
were changing.
The giant
was getting smaller and smaller,
while the dwarf
was getting bigger and bigger.

Not until they were
the same height,
and could look at each other
face to face,
for the very first time,

did the giant stop shrinking,
and the dwarf stop growing.
Their dearest wish had been granted.
They had turned
into Men.

At that very moment,
the magic bird
spread its wings,
rose from its nest,
flew up into the sky,
and never came back.

But ever afterwards,
when the two men
felt like shaking their fists
or putting out their tongues,
a brightly coloured bird
would fly overhead,
reminding them
of the way they used to be.